GW00854423

LiL WAYNE

Takin' The Rap

Publisher and Creative Director: Nick Wells
Project Editors: Polly Prior and Catherine Taylor
Picture Research: Laura Bulbeck and Alex McClean
Art Director and Layout Design: Mike Spender
Digital Design and Production: Chris Herbert

Special thanks to: Stephen Feather, Karen Fitzpatrick and Sara Robson

FLAME TREE PUBLISHING
Crabtree Hall, Crabtree Lane
Fulham, London SW6 6TY
United Kingdom

www.flametreepublishing.com

First published 2012

12 14 16 15 13
1 3 5 7 9 10 8 6 4 2

Flame Tree Publishing is part of The Foundry Creative Media Co. Ltd

A CIP record for this book is available from the British Library upon request.

ISBN 978-0-85775-279-6

Printed in China

LiL WAYNE

Takin' The Rap

MORWENNA FERRIER

FOREWORD: Priya Elan, Assistant Editor, NME.com

**FLAME TREE
PUBLISHING**

CONTENTS

FOREWORD

He might be a record label president and a wannabe rock-star but the many monikered Lil Wayne is a hip-hop artist first and foremost. But Weezy's not just any hip-hop artist. He is someone who has, during his almost 15-year-long career, revolutionized the rap game.

As he moved from the underground to massive mainstream success, Dwayne Michael Carter changed the expectations of what rappers should be like, shying away from the genre's emphasis on big showy, multi-branded hip-hop egos and putting the focus back on the music. He turned his back on the bling, lifestyle aspects of rap and focused instead on the core, old-skool values, specifically creating great inventive rhymes that talked about what was going on in society and mixing these with jaw-dropping beats and sounds.

Wayne's flow is comparable to poetry. His undeniable freestyle talent chopped up metaphors, multiple references and punch lines, and gave the next generation of rappers - particularly his own Cash Money brood of Nicki Minaj and Drake – the confidence and vision to look beyond rap's horizons and continue the evolution of the genre.

Lil Wayne: Taking The Rap tells the extraordinary, colourful story of this musical maverick, from writing his first rap aged 8 to joining the Hot Boyz in the 1990s through to multi-platinum success with his *Tha Carter* series and his multiple re-inventions.

It's a story like no other because Wayne is a true one-off.

Priya Elan, Assistant Editor
www.NME.com

WHO IS LIL WAYNE?

Dwayne Michael Carter, Jr is a man of many names: Weezy, Birdman Junior, Lil Weezy; but above all, Lil Wayne. He is also a man of many guises: after launching his career as a member of rap group Hot Boys in the 1990s, Wayne went on to emerge as a hugely influential solo artist in his own right. His career has gone from hardcore rap to madcap rants to lyrical complexity and as he's changed, so has the music industry and technology around him.

A huge part of Wayne's success has come from internet support instead of radio and TV. Using social networking sites such as Twitter and Facebook, leaking music and even launching a blog after entering jail, Wayne's internet presence has grown to be bigger than any other musician's – without it, he wouldn't be the rapper he is today.

CLIMBING TO THE TOP

Known both for his solo work and for rapping on songs by the likes of Destiny's Child and Mary J. Blige, Wayne has worked with every big name in the business, winning almost every award in the US music industry. He has grossed around £30 million in ticket sales, sold well over 100 million albums worldwide and, in a self-fulfilling prophecy, has become the one thing he always knew he could be: the hottest rapper in the world.

'Anybody who can be explained should be ashamed of themselves. I wasn't created, I wasn't made. I was put here and there's no word for it.'

LIL WAYNE

When you think rappers such as Jay Z, Kanye West and P Diddy are still active in the game, these are big words for a little guy – Wayne is 1.67 m (5 ft 6 in) tall. But, with 14 albums to his name, 11 official mixtapes and a career spanning almost 20 years, and all this at the tender age of 29, he's nothing short of hip-hop royalty.

GETTING RECOGNITION

Although Wayne had been rapping since the mid-1990s, he truly struck gold at the end of 2007, when an MTV poll selected Lil Wayne as Hottest MC in the Game. The same year, *The New Yorker* magazine ranked him Rapper Of The Year.

'Don't stop believing in me. They say I'm the Hottest MC in the Game. If you label me that, I will live up to it. Trust me.'

LIL WAYNE

'I don't want to be the best rapper in the world. If I have a rap album I'm dropping, then I want it to be the best rap album. But I want to be the best.'

LIL WAYNE

Then, in 2008, just as his most popular album – *Tha Carter III* – came out, Wayne was nominated for eight Grammys, the most for any artist nominated that year. He was also named the first ever MTV Man Of The Year. He won the Grammy Award for Best Rap Solo Performance for 'A Milli'; Best Rap Performance by a Duo or Group for his appearance in T.I.'s single 'Swagga Like Us', and Best Rap Song for 'Lollipop'. *Tha Carter III* won the award for Best Rap Album. He was also named 'Best MC' by Rolling Stone.

THE MAN BEHIND THE MUSIC

By 2009, just 10 years after Wayne had started to record as an official artist, MTV named him number two on their list of the Hottest MCs In The Game. Not bad going for a kid born into poverty in New Orleans who worked his way through school, fatherhood, crime, death and on to the stage and infamy.

But, as is often the case, behind every genius is a fascinating backstory and few musicians working right now have had it harder, louder and madder than the pint-sized rapper. Since 1999 Lil Wayne has scored over 60 *Billboard* hits, more than any other rapper in the world today. Is Lil Wayne the hottest rapper alive as he has claimed to be? Possibly. But the real question remains: who is Lil Wayne and how did he get where he is today?

TOUGH BEGINNINGS

Born Dwayne Michael Carter, Jr, on 27 September 1982, in New Orleans, Lil Wayne was brought up in the rough and impoverished Hollygrove neighbourhood of the city's 17th Ward. His mother, Jacita, a chef, was just 19 and married to Dwayne Michael Turner when Wayne was born. But, when Wayne was just two years old, Dwayne Senior abandoned his family. His mother later remarried, although Wayne has rarely mentioned his real father since.

Despite the tough start, Wayne performed well at Lafayette Elementary School, earning himself a place on the Gifted Child Programme. He then won a place at the Eleanor McMain Middle School where he stuck well to his studies, but the truth was his heart was in music. In fact, having written his first rap at the age of 8, as Gangsta D, you could say Wayne was a prodigy.

'Where I **come from,** the block become your **daddy.** There's a lot of **people** get **killed** in **New Orleans** and a lot of **us** be **raised** without a **daddy.'**

LIL WAYNE

GETTING NOTICED

New Orleans was already a hotbed of black music. Well known for producing rhythm and blues artists such as Little Richard and Fats Domino, by the 1990s that genre had grown into hip hop and one label, Cash Money, was a specialist. Naturally, Wayne wanted to ingratiate himself on to the scene.

Aged 11, after tracking down the number of the label's co-owner, Bryan 'Birdman' Williams, Wayne recorded some rhymes on his answering machine and hung around the label's offices hoping to get noticed. Birdman later recalled how he came to notice Wayne: 'Wayne was in front of a record store in New Orleans. When he rapped for me I gave him my card … and he called me. Called me about a hundred times.' Thankfully, the ploy worked. 'So I told him to come down the studio. And he ain't never left me since.'

LEARNING CURVE

On one level, things were looking good for Wayne: he had shown a flair for getting himself noticed and was still excelling at school. By the age of 12 he had even starred in a production of *The Wiz* as the Tin Man. But outside the school gates, he had started to lose interest in his studies. There, Wayne had begun to be tempted into a life of dealing drugs on his local streets. It was only after receiving much-needed attention from Birdman that the future started looking positive.

'I was raised by a single mom. I didn't come from a lot of wealth. I got into my share of trouble as a child. My life could have easily taken a turn for the worse.'

LIL WAYNE

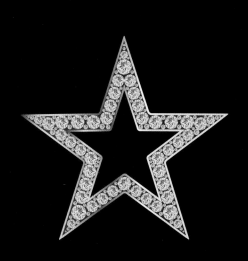

'I found myself at 14, though. My first solo album, I was 14 ... You gotta find yourself in life, period. Once you know who you are, man ...'

LIL WAYNE

Thanks to Birdman's mentoring skills, along with his savvy business sense, Wayne was given the opportunity to do something altogether more constructive: to make music. At 12 years old, he became the youngest rapper ever to sign to the New Orleans hip-hop label and not long after, Wayne started spending serious time at Cash Money Records.

SAVING GRACE

Maybe it was luck that Wayne met the man who would change his life, or maybe it was talent. Either way, Wayne had a knack for dictating his fate. Wayne has never regretted a lifetime growing up on skid row because it shaped him.

Sadly his signing to Cash Money didn't stop him getting into trouble, most notably at 13 when he was playing with his stepfather's 44-calibre handgun and accidentally shot himself, landing him in hospital for a fortnight. He recovered but the incident left a dent on the young rapper's identity. With the help of Birdman, now acting as a sort of father figure when Wayne needed it most, he started concentrating more on the music. And who knows where modern hip hop would be had Birdman not intervened?

A LITTLE AMBITION

By 1994 Lil Wayne was still enrolled at school but doing odd jobs around the office of Cash Money in between writing and rhyming. Until now, Cash Money had made its name by putting out low-budget gangsta rap but Lil Wayne's juvenile rhymes gave a certain swagger, which could set the label apart from its rivals.

So, Birdman and Cash Money's in-house producer, Mannie Fresh, decided to take a chance on the young rapper and Gangsta D (as Lil Wayne was first known) was born.

After including him as a guest on various group recordings just one year after signing him, Mannie partnered Wayne with one of their other young signees, 14-year-old B.G., short for 'Baby Gangsta', and dubbed the rapping duo the B.G.'z. In 1995, the pair of them released an album, *True Story*.

BROTHERS IN ARMS

B.G. and Wayne had become close throughout their teenage years. That same year, Wayne officially took the moniker Lil Wayne, dropping the 'D' from his first name in order to separate himself from an absent father, a big move in Lil Wayne maturing as a person.

'I went from being a rookie – just pure motivation – to noticing that "OK, I'm becoming different". Once I got a whiff of that, it made me keep going.'

LIL WAYNE

For Wayne, however, it was odd to be working in an adult world. He had to grow up quickly. The duo were the youngest rappers signed to a largely adult label and Wayne's mother wasn't happy with his career choice or the profanity of his lyrics. But, true to rebellious form, Wayne continued to rap. Eventually his mother gave in – she knew how much this meant to him – and the pairing proved to be fundamental to Wayne's confidence as an artist. Although B.G. left the label in the late 1990s, he remains for ever part of the Cash Money family.

THE BOYS ARE IN TOWN

One of Lil Wayne's strengths was that he seemed to work well with anyone – despite being much younger. He had a prodigious confidence, something that probably came from him stepping up as father of the family at such a young age.

It certainly proved a useful tool when Lil Wayne and B.G. set to work on a new, all-star rap collective, which proved to be a decisive part of Wayne's rise to fame. In 1997 Hot Boys, a hardcore teenage rap group he formed with B.G. alongside fellow Louisiana rappers Juvenile and Young Turk, was born and established Cash Money Records as a label that specialized in southern hip hop.

At the age of 15, Carter was the youngest member at that time but probably the most gifted: his rolling rhymes and distinctive voice set him apart from the other members. The boy would go far.

'When it was time to sing with the guys, I knew exactly what to say and do. But when it was time for someone to hear me rap, then you was going to get something different.' LIL WAYNE

PLAYING THE MAINSTREAM

In 1997, Hot Boys released their debut, *Get It How U Live*, and the album sold remarkably well for an unknown debut, peaking at around 400,000. They had garnered a big following, playing sellout shows in Louisiana and earning their keep on the Cash Money payroll.

Finally, Wayne left school and in 1999 it was announced that Cash Money had signed a deal with the label Universal to distribute work by Hot Boys. Under the watchful eye of Mannie and Birdman, the foursome recorded *Guerilla Warfare*, which reached No. 1 on the *Billboard* magazine Top R&B/Hip-Hop Albums chart.

That the group went on to break up in 2001 was of little importance. Despite forming his career on the streets of New Orleans, Wayne had reached the mainstream. Just 17 years old but three albums down, rapper extraordinaire Lil Wayne was the one to watch.

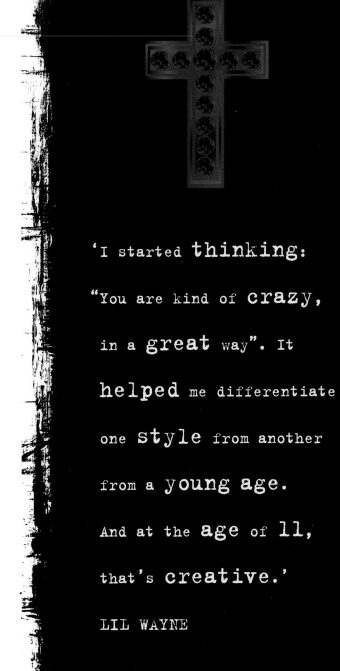

'I started thinking: "You are kind of crazy, in a great way". It helped me differentiate one style from another from a young age. And at the age of 11, that's creative.' LIL WAYNE

DOING IT ALONE

After the success of Hot Boys, Wayne was determined to cement his status as a mature MC – but solo. It was a risky time. Hot Boys had been selling well and Wayne didn't want to seem egotistical. But deep down Wayne knew that, in order to make it, he had to forge a career on his own.

His first album, *Tha Block is Hot* (1999)*,* came out while Wayne was still with Hot Boys, and featured group members on more than half of the album's 17 songs. The record was produced by Cash Money's very own Mannie, so hopes were high; but despite the label's financial backing it was a commercial flop. Dubbed 'lyrically aggressive', it seemed mainstream America wasn't ready for Wayne's hardcore rhymes. He was devastated. He had the right clique, the right producer – all at just 18. Surely success was due?

FINDING OUT THE HARD WAY

Lil Wayne was no quitter though. Undeterred by his first album, he redeemed himself with the subsequent two albums: *Lights Out* (2000), and *500 Degreez* (2002). Both went gold, a first for Wayne, but he still had a lot to prove to his critics who criticized him for rapping like a teenager. To make matters worse, back home things were falling apart.

'You're **introduced** to the **streets** of **New Orleans** at a **young** age. **Nobody** ever looked at **me** as a little **kid rapper** – just a **bad ass** kid. I'm a **man** now.'

LIL WAYNE

With 9/11 in the recent background and Wall Street subsequently crashing, rumours began circulating about Cash Money's own financial troubles and potential demise. The rest of Hot Boys had left the label and while Wayne remained, his planned 2003 album was scrapped owing to financial problems.

At this point, most artists would have given up, but not Wayne. He decided to do something that would change the face of music, and his career, like nothing else.

'I wanted to try to help us get off the block. That was my goal because I watched my brothers and our pops go to penitentiary and get killed.'

LIL WAYNE

MAKING THE BRAND

Rather than abandon it, Wayne decided to release the album as a mixtape named *Da Drought*. It was well received but what's more, it was a great move by the rapper: as of yet, no major artist had used mixtapes to such an effect. Having shown the world that he was capable of succeeding in the face of adversity, he set about rebuilding his brand, The Carter, and in 2004 released his self-named album, *Tha Carter*, marking what critics called an advancement in both his style and themes. Gone were the childish raps about women. Now Wayne was talking about being 'a grown man'. The album sold over 1 million copies in the US, while single 'Go DJ' became a Top 5 hit. How did he know he'd arrived? He was asked to rap on Destiny's Child's single 'Soldier'. And it didn't get bigger than that.

SEAL THE DEAL

One thing was for sure: in the space of under 10 years Lil Wayne had grown up. His fifth and follow-up album, *Tha Carter II* (2005), secured his reputation as a mature artist. It sold more than 238,000 copies in its first week of release and went on to sell 2 million copies worldwide.

His voice had become deeper and growly, his on-stage antics more theatrical. But he had also shown that, despite a series of flops, if you want it you have to fight for it and now the little kid from New Orleans had made it in America. No wonder he dubbed himself the greatest rapper alive on this album. That summer of 2005 was Lil Wayne's breakout time. He was riding high. Then, just before Labor Day, the unthinkable happened back home: Hurricane Katrina.

'Everything that everyone see and notice, those things happen one day, one week, those things happen whenever. But I work every single day. I work every single hour.'

LIL WAYNE

THE HURRICANE EFFECT

Just months before Wayne's album, *Tha Carter II*, was released Hurricane Katrina hit Louisiana with devastating effect. Causing severe destruction along the coast from central Florida to Texas, the most significant death toll occurred in Lil Wayne's home city, New Orleans, flooding after the outdated levee system failed. Around 80 per cent of the city and surrounding areas were flooded catastrophically, and the floodwaters lingered for weeks. Yet no one came to its rescue.

'Hurricane Katrina, we should've called it Hurricane Bush. Then they telling y'all lies on the news. The white people smiling like everything cool. But I know people that died in that pool.'

LIL WAYNE

For Wayne, this proved devastating. Although Wayne had since moved to Miami, he lost his New Orleans home and a significant number of friends and even distant family. He became a vocal critic of the aftermath, criticizing the government's lack of concern, and decided to use his music to provoke a reaction among the public. Katrina, it seemed, spurred on Wayne's creativity and in return he rallied for support.

A FORCE FOR GOOD

A few months after Katrina hit, Wayne started the first of many Katrina-inspired projects. First came *Dedication 2*, a mixtape that paired Lil Wayne with DJ Drama, and contained the socially conscious track 'Georgia Bush', a brilliant blending of Ray Charles's 'Georgia On My Mind' with Lil Wayne's own lyrics, in which he criticized the way then-US President George W. Bush responded to the effects of Hurricane Katrina. It was a celebrated mixtape, appearing on a vast number of Top 10 album lists. Wayne also wrote the song 'Tie My Hands' with soul singer Robin Thicke, a track that contained a very obvious commentary about the incompetence of the US government: 'No governor, no help from the mayor'. Critically acclaimed and released to a more mainstream audience, the duo's performance at the 2007 Grammys was met with a standing ovation.

RISE OF THE SOUTH

Hurricane Katrina and Wayne's furious reaction were pivotal moments in the rapper's success and musical style. Up until

'I believe that music is another form of news. Music is another form of journalism to me so I have to cover all the areas with my album.'

LIL WAYNE

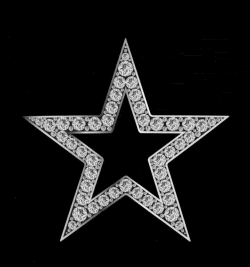

'When you **tell** them what to **do**, that's when they get **angry** when you tell them be **like me** because it's **hard** to be **like me**.'

LIL WAYNE

now, the south of the States had been about country music or (unknown to most) Bounce music, an energetic style of New Orleans hip hop that influenced Lil Wayne's style throughout his career. Until now, New Orleans rap had no musical identity, and in the eyes of the rest of the world, no musical unity. New Orleans was segregated from the rest of America, culturally and racially. The disaster did a lot of damage but for music it provided a new scene, and at its forefront was Lil Wayne. In terms of black music, East Coast and West Coast had been all anyone talked about. But now there was a new coast down south and one with a deep political agenda.

THE GREAT CLEAR-UP

In the aftermath of the hurricane, Lil Wayne was a key benefactor in the city's regeneration. He was reported to have donated $200,000 to the development of his old playground destroyed by the floods. He also made a film with Tim Story called *Tie My Hands*, which showed the effects of the storm.

Universally, the hurricane and the resulting creative output gave authority to a unified black voice and Lil Wayne was at its helm. For Wayne personally though, Katrina was key in channelling a mature style. His past lyrics had covered women, guns and crime; however, now new themes were beginning to emerge, about how his life had been carved from poverty, the absence of his father and the people he had lost. He was starting to address police brutality, government corruption – a voice of New Orleans people.

A SENSE OF STYLE

Having matured in his subject matter by 2006, Lil Wayne took this opportunity to explore new types of word-play and various vocal techniques. Every rapper is defined by his voice – Jay Z by his authoritative tones, Kanye West by his soft abstract vocals – and Wayne wanted to do the same. In the past, his ability to rhyme quickly had set him apart from other rappers, but there was only so far pace would take him. So he started adopting new rap voices. He would work hard into the night trying out different techniques, and out of his practice grew the strangled Daffy Duck voice, the robot voice and his gravelly growling whisper. He showcased his hard work at a performance at New York's Beacon Theater in 2008. The audience was stunned as each voice came and went and, importantly, both critics and crowds loved it.

GOOD HAIR DAYS

This new rapping style combined with *Tha Carter* and its follow-up transformed Wayne from a teenage ghetto rapper to a mainstream player, so it was high time Lil Wayne forged a whole look to go with his new-found fame. Since he was 15 years old, Wayne had been growing his hair into dreadlocks, a look that stayed true to his black urban roots. The dreads appeared on numerous Hot Boys videos and later, cropped, on the cover of *Tha Carter*. By *Tha Carter II*, they were in pride of place as Wayne posed triumphantly alongside a Hummer.

His hair had become part and parcel of Lil Wayne: 'My dreads hang to let him know that I'm a lion. Represent the jungle when the others just trying.' More importantly, he was one of the first rappers to have a truly individual style.

BLING BLING

Wayne's teeth – or grills – were one of Wayne's first big extravagances and they have become his most infamous statement. Exactly why he decided to encrust his teeth with gold and diamonds is unknown – after all, they have caused all manner of problems. He has to brush them after every meal with specialist toothpaste and they are prone to infections, often compounded by the jewels because they make his teeth hard to clean. Still, Lil Wayne maintains they are as much part of him as anything else. It is certainly a statement: Wayne had been saving up for them since the 1990s, when they became coveted accessories for rappers.

And since Lil Wayne is the man credited with inventing the term 'bling bling' way back in 1997 when he was a teenage rapper, diamond teeth are about as bling as it gets, especially with a price tag of around $150,000.

'I'm **not gonna** say I don't know what will **happen** before I **say** it on **record.** I **do know** what **will** happen. I am **aware** of it. It **is** what it is.' LIL WAYNE

'I'ma die with these.
So these are my teeth.
I can go to the dentist
and switch them out,
but it's surgery.'

LIL WAYNE

PAINTED MAN

Perhaps Lil Wayne's greatest statement is his tattoos. It is believed he has somewhere between 200 and 300 over his entire anatomy, each telling a tale, with the most important ones being the most unusual. Take the prayer on his back, showing his adoption of religion, and below that, a map of Louisiana to represent his roots, while on his shoulder he has a bird, representing his surrogate father, 'Birdman'. On his chest, there is a Cash Money tattoo for his first label and next to that, a 17-inch tattoo that represents the 17th ward of New Orleans where Wayne grew up. On his arms are the words 'Nae Nae', the name of his daughter, and on his face, stars and teardrops, for the people in his family who have been killed. Tattoos might not be for everyone, but for Wayne they are a form of expression.

'My first tattoo is
this tattoo right here, in
memory of rabbit, it's
up to me. That's my dad.
He passed when I was
14, so I got it when I
was 14. These tattoos
don't rub off.'

LIL WAYNE

hixing it up

Lil Wayne had been making mixtapes since 2003 when he released a scrapped album as *Dedication*. But even when he peaked into the mainstream in the mid-2000s, he continued to produce a steady flow of high-quality mixes available to download on iTunes. For Wayne, they proved that the age-old methods of distribution no longer ruled the world of hip hop. It also meant he could bypass regular promotion and use Facebook (and later Twitter) to market them, making him one of the first to do so.

The most popular were *Dedication* and *Dedication 2* (2006). They were compilations containing original tracks dotted with 'mash-ups' in which Lil Wayne recorded new lyrics over another beat. Some critics believe they contain his best work and in 2007, US *GQ* named him Man Of The Year on the strength of his mixes.

LEAKY BEATS

Wayne continued to release his albums on Universal while his mixtapes went online, but as to whether his songs were leaked on to the internet by mistake is unknown. Understandably, Universal were up in arms when parts of Lil Wayne's sixth album, *Tha Carter III* (2008), found their way on to fan sites.

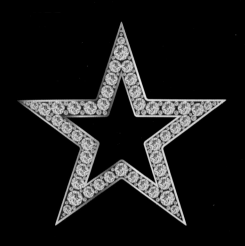

'On **mixtapes** I say **whatever** comes to mind. That ain't **freestyle** ... 'cause **freestyling** is **dumb** to me. Not the **battling** they do on DVDs and stuff, they be **rapping** for **real** ...'

LIL WAYNE

'I'll **probably** just collect all the SONGS that's floating around and make my own **mixtape** called The Leak since people want the music so bad.'

LIL WAYNE

Wayne was forced to change the track listing and release the leaked tracks, plus four new ones, on a separate 2007 EP, *The Leak*. Never one to miss an opportunity though, he also distributed some of the leaked tracks on mixtapes, which he named *The Drought Is Over Pt. 2* and *The Drought Is Over Pt. 4*. It was an unprecedented move for the rapper but something which won Wayne a new underground fanbase and a good reception from *Rolling Stone*. One of the leaked albums, *Da Drought 3,* was even hailed as the best mixtape of 2007 by MTV News.

THIRD TIME LUCKY?

The year 2008 was a difficult one for black music. Hip hop was on the decline, indie rock was at an all-time high in the charts (MGMT and Vampire Weekend both released debuts that year), and with a substantial portion of Wayne's sixth album, *Tha Carter III,* appearing online prematurely, many rappers would have bowed out of releasing an album. But not Lil Wayne. Determined to make the rest of the album a success, he released the re-edited album the following year.

Such was the anticipation of this album that Wayne's gamble paid off – it bucked all trends and sold more than a million copies in its first week, going on to sell a further 2 million copies, earning Wayne eight Grammy Award nominations. It was an unorthodox method but still, *Tha Carter III* was his best album to date.

THE GREATEST OF THEM ALL

As an album, *Tha Carter III* was head and shoulders above anything else he had done previously. Not only did it place an underground rapper squarely in the mainstream, a rapper to rival the likes of 50 Cent and Eminem, but it did so with real Southern style. The album was a combination of hardcore rap, truly surreal beats and pop, and featured some of the biggest names in the genre: Kanye West, Jay Z, Babyface and singer Robin Thicke, with whom he recorded the lauded Katrina single, 'Tie My Hands'. The album went on to become the fastest-selling album of the year in the US and the Facebook love poured in.

It also contained the single 'Lollipop', Wayne's most commercially successful song at that point, making it the first Top 10 single for Lil Wayne as a solo artist. Finally, Wayne was playing with the big boys.

'People got to understand there's **no peak** on **record** selling, there's **no limit,** so you never reach your **goal,** you're never **satisfied.** And I **expected** to **sell** that **much.'**
LIL WAYNE

DREAM TEAM WORK

Lil Wayne had cemented his solo career and become a household name, but he was bored and eager to branch out and work with new artists. By the time *Tha Carter III* had come out, Lil Wayne had started collaborating with everyone and anyone in the business. The success from his cameo on the Destiny's Child track 'Soldier' in 2004 made him the go-to guy for rhymes, but he kept his collaborations as unusual and genre-defying as ever. Lil Wayne went on to rap on Madonna's track 'Revolver', a Weezer song 'Can't Stop Partying', and then returned to his roots, rhyming with Chris Brown on 'Gimme That' and Wyclef Jean's 'Sweetest Girl (Dollar Bill)'. By far his best work was achieved with soul singer Robin Thicke on 'Tie My Hands', with Wayne's gruff rhymes working well with Robin's dulcet tones.

UNIVERSAL HOPES

As big a success as Wayne had become, he had also started coming to blows with his label, Universal, who were struggling to keep up with his output. Although they got to OK every cameo, they were keen for him to record another album and fought hard to rein him in. Wayne, however, wanted to experiment with singing, rock and pop. Universal were frustrated. Tensions between both parties were rising until, one day in 2005, Wayne came up with a plan that would keep Universal sweet and allow him to explore new music.

'If you make **everything** you do **great**, like I **do** ... no **lie**, man. It's like, "You want **Michael Jordan** on your **team?**" "Hell **yeah!** Yeah, I want him on my **team, stupid**".'
LIL WAYNE

Having worked his way through the ranks from Cash Money's tea boy to group rapper to major solo artist, Wayne was finally able to give something back to the music industry that nurtured him. He set up his own label with the backing of Universal.

ONE BIG FAMILY

In 2005, Wayne founded Young Money Entertainment, an imprint of his beloved Cash Money Records and distributed by Universal. This new label would be a sort of foundation for talented new hip-hop artists and luckily Universal were one hundred per cent behind him.

He signed a variety of artists including Jae Millz, Mack Maine, Tyga and Gudda Gudda who all became part of the We Are Young Money Crew, recording a collaborative album under Wayne's watchful eye and even touring as a group and releasing a collective album. By 2007 Lil Wayne had handed management of Young Money over to his old friend and manager, Cortez Bryant, but these artists were made for life. We Are Young Money was Wayne's new family and he was their father. And he sure as hell wasn't going to let them down.

YOUNG PRODIGIES

Of all Young Money's artists, two stood out: Nicki Minaj and Drake. Raised in New York, Nicki's upbringing was problematic: her father was a drug addict who used to sell

'Drake is my artist ... He's not just a friend. We're more than friends. It's business. It would be impossible for it to be a competition. I mean, I'm the guy's boss.'
LIL WAYNE

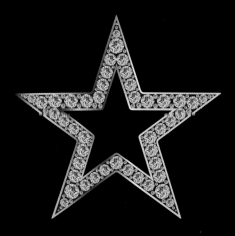

the family's belongings to fund his habit. Until now Nicki worked in bars to save money for studio time but it wasn't long before one track made its way to Lil Wayne, who signed her on the spot. She's now one of the most talked-about artists of 2011.

Like Nicki, Toronto-born Drake had a difficult upbringing. However, unlike many hip-hop artists, Aubrey Drake Graham wasn't interested in the gangsta life. In fact, it was Drake's gentle side that persuaded Wayne to sign him; he would often tell Drake to 'be the guy that I could never be'. Drake took his advice and went on to win *GQ* Man Of The Year in 2010.

'I just thought she [Nicki] was going to be the new female MC that none of these other female MCs can touch, but now, she's blossomed into a megastar with this new attitude and style.'

LIL WAYNE

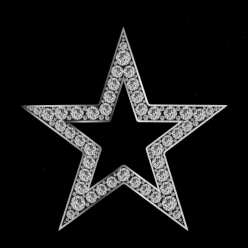

TIME FOR REINVENTION

When Lil Wayne declared himself the 'best rapper alive,' no one was surprised. After all, he seemed to live up to that moniker on his 'Tha Carter' series. But then something changed. It was 2009, and Wayne was taking time out to work on his new record, *Rebirth*, when a track called 'Prom Queen' leaked on to the internet. Leaking tracks was nothing new – plenty of Wayne's songs had been leaked in the past – but this song sounded like heavy metal. There was no rapping, no rhyming, just loud, screeching guitars and what sounded like Lil Wayne singing. The Facebook reaction was excited but also confused. Surely, it was a hoax – no artist in his right mind would switch genres from rap to rock at the pinnacle of his career? But then this was Lil Wayne – anything was possible.

ROCKING ALL OVER THE WORLD

In an interview with *Rolling Stone*, Wayne explained that as his celebrity status took off, he was starting to experience a life unlike anything he could rap about – so he switched to rock. Why? Because he was Lil Wayne and he could do what he wanted.

'I always knew I couldn't sing, but I also knew I had a voice that isn't heard by many and that I could learn how to stretch it and make songs sound good.'

LIL WAYNE

His fans should have guessed: Wayne had spent the last 12 months making the odd appearance on stage with an electric guitar, most notably at the 2008 Country Music Awards, where Wayne hopped on stage with rocker Kid Rock to perform a remix of 'All Summer Long'. His label had previously made a statement that Lil Wayne was the first hip-hop act to perform at the awards at the time, but it seemed like a one-off. Little did his fans know that it was only the beginning of a genre-change that would divide the hip-hop world.

SECOND BIRTH?

In early 2010 Lil Wayne announced that *Rebirth* would be a rock album. His fans were bemused – his last rap album, *Tha Carter III*, was his biggest commercial success to date. MTV had just made Lil Wayne No. 2 on their 2009 list of the 'Hottest MCs In The Game.' What was Wayne up to?

The album suffered several delays but eventually it came out in February 2010. The cover would see Wayne reclining on a throne with a guitar. He even roped in help from his new friend Pete Wentz from Fall Out Boy, and recorded the track 'Drop The World' with Eminem, a good choice since Eminem had previously made the rap-rock crossover on *The Marshall Mathers LP* (2000). Why couldn't Wayne match his success? But as Wayne was to find out, mixing genres is notoriously hit-and-miss: it barely went gold.

'I never said, "Lil Wayne is going to rock, everybody." I just got – I'm not going to say "so good" at what I was doing, but it became such a regularity for me.'

LIL WAYNE

i'm only human

The year 2010 would prove to be a difficult one for Wayne. His attempt to change genre failed and a series of unrelated court appearances left the rapper troubled about his personal life. For once, Wayne did the right thing and in 2010 he abandoned his new direction and recorded his eighth album, *I Am Not A Human Being*. It would define the Young Money style, and even start a Twitter meme in its name. It wasn't his best work but it was well-structured gentle Southern Bounce and the sound was certainly preferable to his previous attempt to rock out. To the critics, however, it had the markings of a man who had played with fire – and got burned. After all, by the time the album was released Wayne had been sent to prison. The big question was whether Wayne's fans would forgive him *Rebirth* or forget him in prison.

'I go wherever my creativity takes me. I ain't gotta be in no zone, 'cause if I was in a zone, I ain't never fall out. I ain't never out of the zone.'

LIL WAYNE

'I wanna let you know that New Orleans was truly the birthplace of my career. Y'all were the first people to f*©k with my music, and I recognize that.'

LIL WAYNE

A REAL ROLE MODEL

Throughout his career, Lil Wayne has used his music to describe the dynamic of 'the hood' where he grew up, the ongoing struggles of his native New Orleans and crime in America's inner cities to outsiders. In later years he even discussed Barack Obama's bid to become the first black President.

But now, with the Young Money Crew established as one of hip hop's most exciting new labels of talent, Lil Wayne was aware of his new-found status: as a role model. As much as Wayne loved his public persona, he wasn't comfortable with this – it was one thing to tell it like it is but another thing to have his every action scrutinized. In fact, as far as he was concerned, Wayne was a positive father figure for his two young children and that was it.

HELPING OUT BACK HOME

Wayne faced little choice: he was a public figure and so instead he capitalized on this role by setting up the One Family Foundation in New Orleans. Seeking to empower urban youth by providing opportunities to cultivate their talents and skills, he wanted to give New Orleans' kids the chance he never had. In addition, these kids would also learn to be self-sufficient, to work, to look after their family, all while being motivated to become successful. With a strong focus on family orientation, Wayne's charity gave stability to those who needed it most. One of its biggest achievements was to

restore Harrel Park in the 17th Ward of New Orleans, destroyed in Hurricane Katrina. The new, improved facility consists of a track and field, basketball court, children's playground and pool, facilities this part of New Orleans could previously only dream of.

'Before I go, I think it's amazing what's been done for Haiti ... but I also think it's amazing what hasn't been done for New Orleans.'

LIL WAYNE

PRESIDENTIAL BACKING

Unsurprisingly, Wayne's efforts to instil good values into his hometown caught the attention of the newly elected President Barack Obama.

The President admitted to being a fan of the New Orleans rapper, explaining in an interview: 'Jay-Z used to be sort of what predominated, but now I've got a little Nas and a

little Lil Wayne.' Naturally Wayne was thrilled: Barack Obama, one of his childhood role models, a man he's publicly and vocally backed, was a fan.

However, Barack Obama was also acutely aware of the dangers of Wayne becoming a role model, primarily because of his success. Since the age of 11, Lil Wayne had overcome every hurdle to become a self-made multimillion dollar earning artist. And, as Obama mentioned in his inauguration speech, not every black kid in America had the ability to do the same.

TELLING IT LIKE IT IS

Wayne's philanthropic efforts didn't go unnoticed by the music industry either. So when a catastrophic earthquake hit the island of Haiti in 2010, the music world came to its rescue – and roped in Lil Wayne. Over 50 world-famous and diverse artists, including Tony Bennett and Justin Bieber, sang a chorus of the 2010 remake of the 1985 USA for Africa all-star song, 'We Are The World', in a bid to raise money. What is more, Wayne was asked to cover the line sung by Bob Dylan on the original. When asked if he thought he bettered Dylan's original performance Wayne responded modestly: 'Hell no.' However, he also used the opportunity to make a very public statement about the parallels between Haiti and Katrina, in which he highlighted the fact that no one cared as much about New Orleans as they did about Haiti.

'I was like, "What am I doing here?" But after I did Bob Dylan's part, it kind of hit me that I guess this is way more important than I could ever imagine.'

LIL WAYNE

PLAYING WITH FIRE

In 10 years, Wayne had gone from being just another kid from a broken home to the most talked-about rapper of the decade. But it was during his most successful period that people started to talk about him – for the wrong reasons.

It all started in the summer of 2006. Lil Wayne was on tour to promote his album and was watching TV in his hotel room in Atlanta. Suddenly, there was a knock at the door – it was hotel management saying they had received a few complaints about a strange smell coming from his room. Wayne ignored the complaints and management went away. Soon after, the door knocked again but this time it was the police who entered to find a few samples of medication in the room. It turned out even Lil Wayne wasn't above the law.

JUS' MISBEHAVING

It was Wayne's first public run-in with the law but was to be the first of several: after being arrested he posted bail but months later was arrested in Idaho for a felony-fugitive charge and missed a concert, which saw him run into more trouble with concert organizers. The case was dismissed and both Universal and Wayne, relieved to think they had heard the last of it, went back to business. How wrong they were.

The following summer, Wayne had just headlined his first ever concert at New York's Beacon Theater. The concert was a hit. Wayne was buzzing. The future looked bright. But then the unthinkable happened: leaving the after-party, Wayne's tour bus was pulled over by police and searched. Among his possessions, they found drugs and a gun. Faced with little choice, they arrested Wayne on charges of felony and gun possession.

DAMAGE LIMITATIONS

Following the charges, Wayne was scheduled to return to New York for a status hearing and sentencing. Universal hit the roof and Wayne promised to stop; however, months later his tour bus was pulled over yet again by border-patrol agents in Arizona. A search found more drugs in his possession and although he pleaded not guilty, the damage was done. But Wayne was no fool. Despite the huge media backlash, he realized he had become more famous than ever before – even if it was for the wrong reasons. So, Wayne did the only thing he could do, the only thing he had ever done – he turned a bad situation into a good one, and used the publicity to promote his single 'Lollipop'. It worked: 'Lollipop' reached No. 1 in June 2008, and preceded the huge success of *Tha Carter III*.

'Well, I'm a man. I believe as a man, you should know that. Every man should know the repercussions and consequences behind whatever they do before they do it.'

LIL WAYNE

'This is **Lil Wayne** going to **jail. Nobody** I can **talk** to can **tell me** what that's like. I just **say** I'm **looking forward** to it.'

LIL WAYNE

PAYING HIS DUES

The damage was done: charged with possession, Wayne was sentenced to 12 months inside. Due to enter in February 2010, just when *Rebirth* was due out, this was delayed until March because of dental problems. Having undergone eight root canals, his next hearing was postponed yet again – this time due to a fire in the courthouse. It proved to be a torturous period for Wayne who just wanted to get prison over with. Finally, it was announced that he would enter Rikers Island, just off New York, on 8 March. In the run-up to his incarceration, Wayne recorded over 30 videos for his fans and spent his final night with his Cash Money Records crew at a party at the Liv Club in Miami, hosted by Birdman. The cake read 'Keep Your Head Up Weezy'. It was all he could do.

'I can **capitalize** on my **mistakes** and **make** the **best** next **move.** It's not interesting for the **world** unless you're **writing** a **book** or something. And you **know** how I **feel** about **books.**' LIL WAYNE

A LIFE INSIDE

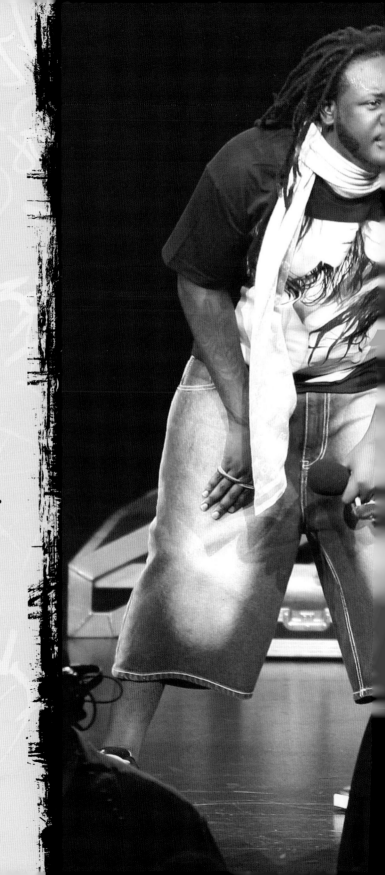

Few people would be pleased to go to jail, but for Lil Wayne his fears were far more career-defining. For his own safety, Wayne was to be housed in a unit specifically built to house inmates classified as 'too vulnerable for the general population'. But a bigger problem was entering jail at the prime of his career. He had started to forge a huge online presence using Facebook and also set up his Twitter account – but would his fans now desert him? Luckily, Wayne had a team of people who would keep up his dialogue with the outside world. He set up his blog, Weezythanxyou, on which his team would periodically post Wayne's letters and blogs about his daily Rikers routine as well as new songs he had heard on the radio. He also did his utmost to reply to as much fan mail that flooded his cell as was possible.

'I'm **prepared** for any situation. I've **never** been afraid of anything but **God**. I look at it as an **experience**. I say I'm **looking forward** to it.'

LIL WAYNE

'I laughed with some of you, reasoned with some of you, and even cried with some of you. I never imagined how much impact my words and life can have.'

LIL WAYNE

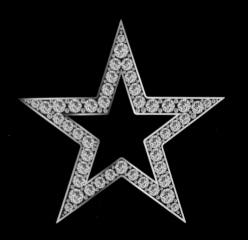

BEST OF A BAD SITUATION

Wayne also had an album to release … while he was inside. It was a logistical nightmare so he turned to one of his few long-standing friends, Cortez Bryant, who had befriended Wayne when he was 15 years old and Wayne was 12, pushed him into after-school music programmes and became his manager. After all, Wayne had already handed over his label, Young Money, to Cortez in 2007.

Bryant was one of the sanest people Wayne knew. Under Cortez's watchful eye, Cash Money released Wayne's rock album, *Rebirth*, just before he was sentenced, and steamed ahead on the promotion. It was Cortez who made him record over 30 videos to accompany each song, which would be released while Wayne was in jail. With everything set up, Wayne wrote his first letter to fans, 'Gone 'til November', and like that he went to Rikers.

NEW YEAR, NEW MEDIA

With Wayne inside, Cortez moved Young Money from Miami to New York so the pair of them could liaise and build Wayne's presence on the internet. During the first half of his imprisonment, Wayne used his blog to its full potential: he published letters, sold Free Weezy T-shirts and wrote songs to appear on Drake's new album, which he would then record over the phone during his allocated phone time.

His Twitter page was also updated regularly, each tweet written in a 'Weezy' style. Cortez meanwhile hired a team of people to help respond to fan letters sent to Wayne and update his Facebook. It was starting to work: a real sense of community had formed. On Facebook alone Wayne had earned 30 million-plus fans, earning him a spot in the Guinness Book of World Records for the most likes in one day.

TIME FOR SOLITUDE

Things were looking up: the blog was a hit and Lil Wayne had just had his sentence slashed because of good behaviour. Suddenly, it all went wrong. Just one month before his release, Wayne made the unwise decision to smuggle in an MP3 player and charger, and hide them inside a crisps packet in his bin. Within days the authorities had spotted the contraband and Wayne was placed in The Bing – solitary confinement. For one month, he spent 23 hours a day in his cell, allowed out only for showers and visitors. He was allowed just one phone call a week (which put an end to his telephone recordings) and one hour a day of 'recreation time', forcing Wayne to sign off Twitter. But this period did have one good outcome: it opened him up to religion, with Lil Wayne, already Catholic, re-finding God.

'Jail didn't make me find God, He's always been there. They can lock me up, but my spirit and my love can never be confined to prison walls.' LIL WAYNE

INTO THE LIMELIGHT

While Wayne's private life was proving to be a rollercoaster, he was also dealing with his public persona. After the success of *Tha Carter III*, he found himself in even greater public demand, getting stopped on the street by fans and chased into his car by women after concerts. He was a true celebrity and, unsurprisingly, Lil Wayne loved it.

The more concerts he did, the more confident he became in front of the cameras. He was appearing regularly on chat shows, most notably *The Jimmy Kimmel Show*, *The Letterman Show* and *The Mo'Nique Show*, where he would discuss his career. He also became a regular on coveted comic show *Saturday Night Live*, performing with fellow rapper Eminem and even participating in scripted skits with Olympic swimmer Michael Phelps. He was becoming as famous as he had once hoped.

PLAYING THE GAME

But as he became more popular, he also grew more lax about how he came across. In early 2009, he participated in a major interview with Katie Couric for CBS's Grammy Special which was decidedly frank – they discussed bowling, his childhood, Hurricane Katrina, why he dropped the 'D' from his real name to become Wayne, his work process and becoming a father. Also, more dangerously, he revealed his love of cough syrup and marijuana, a revelation which sent ripples throughout the media for weeks to come.

'I'm actually **infatuated** and **in love** with what I **do**, therefore **I am** what **I do**. So I never have to **forget** because **I never have** to **remember**, I just **am**.'

LIL WAYNE

Things really came to a head when the father of three was asked if he was a good role model, to which he wasn't sure how to reply. Lil Wayne has always maintained he is a role model to his children only. And this question, in light of his comments about drugs, threw Lil Wayne for six.

TOO MUCH INFORMATION

Next came the ultimate honour – someone wanted to make a film about Lil Wayne and not just anyone – Quincy Jones III, son of the infamous record producer. It would be a documentary shadowing the rapper, 'a labour of love' thought Wayne, agreeing to dismiss the idea of a typical documentary in favour of a more raw look at his life. Quincy then decided against interviews with the rapper in favour of a microphone capturing his every word.

Called *The Carter*, the documentary portrays the rapper on and off stage, the way he deals with his fans and entourage, as well as showing Wayne's addiction to cough syrup. He has rapped repeatedly about his love of the prescription cough medicine, even stating that he would love 'weed and syrup till I die'. Naturally, the documentary led Lil Wayne straight to the firing line.

MIXED BLESSINGS

Prior to its first screening, Wayne was invited to the first ever private showing. He was beyond excited. His life, immortalized.

'But my job is to rap, and I be Lil Wayne. I don't know if you been on other video sets, but it's hard to see that artist become whatever they not.'

LIL WAYNE

But upon seeing the film in the cold light of day, he was horrified. He looked like a drug-addled, fame-hungry monster.

He immediately launched a lawsuit to prevent the release of the film – claiming producers had broken a contract giving him control over the final edit of the documentary. But his request was rejected. To Lil Wayne's horror, the film was still released.

For his fans though, it was a different story. They loved seeing the real Lil Wayne, bare, raw and uncut. The film also showed Wayne's sharp work ethic, which allows him to make such quantities of music so that the public don't have to wait around. For his fans, it was a real insight into who their favourite artist really was.

'I don't like to try to think like **everybody** else, don't like to do nothing everybody else **think** I'm **gone do,** don't like to say nothing **everybody** else think I'm gone say.'

LIL WAYNE

REAL FATHER FIGURE

Family has always played a key role in Lil Wayne's life, mainly because his own was so fractured. After his father abandoned the family, Wayne was raised by his stepfather. But tragedy struck again when he was abducted and shot dead.

It is without doubt due to this lack of a father figure that Wayne formed close relationships with some of his mentors, Cortez Bryant, producer Freshie and, of course, Birdman. After all, it was Birdman who, along with his brother, set up Cash Money records, and Birdman who discovered Carter in 1993 when he was just 11 years old.

The two have a bond so strong that Birdman refers to Wayne simply as 'my son'. They even recorded a compilation album, *Like Father And Son*, which gave Wayne and Birdman an opportunity to publicly express the friendship of their relationship.

LOVE'S YOUNG DREAM

As we all know, behind every successful man is a good woman. And in Lil Wayne's case, there seemed to be quite a few. However, as is often the case with celebrities, only a handful of the women who came forward to say they dated Lil Wayne actually had relations with the rapper.

His first love was childhood sweetheart Antonia Toya Carter. The lovers met when Wayne was aged 15 and at middle school. Wayne used to perform music to Toya's class, something that impressed a then-14-year-old Toya: the boy had talent. It was during Toya's seventh grade year that they started dating and quite soon after, Toya got pregnant. The pair married in 2004 on Valentine's Day only to divorce two years later. It was a brief but formative relationship for Wayne, because Toya was also the mother of his first child.

'I've grown into this person. I woke up one morning and had three or four women in my bed where I not only didn't know their last names, I didn't know the beginning letter of their first names.' LIL WAYNE

PLAYING HAPPY FAMILIES

Wayne later dated Sarah B, a student at Cincinnati University, who gave birth to Wayne's second child, Dwayne Carter III, in 2008, but the romance was fleeting. The second major

'One that still appears on everybody's songs, one that still sounds better than any rapper rapping. One that has four kids and is the greatest father ever to the kids.' LIL WAYNE

relationship in Lil Wayne's life was with the actress Lauren London. Wayne met Lauren when she was 15 years old, but they didn't hook up until much later. It was a fraught relationship – both were ambitiously working on their careers and their relationship was on/off for several years, even getting engaged at one point before calling it all off. Despite that, the couple remain close, especially after the birth of Lennox Samuel Ari in 2009. But his most recent relationship has been with R&B singer Nivea, also the mother of his fourth child Neal, born in November 2009. Of course, the woman who truly shaped Lil Wayne was his mother, Jacita.

THE KIDS ARE ALRIGHT

Wayne has always maintained that he wanted to be a good role model to his four children. His oldest daughter, Reginae, remains a pivotal part of Wayne's life, thanks to her parents' relatively friendly relationship, post-divorce. She has a good relationship with her father, tweeting 'Like Father Like Daughter' on her last birthday when the pair went out for food. She currently appears in reality TV show *TOYA: A Family Affair*, which follows her mother Toya and family on a day-to-day basis.

Reginae is said to take after her father and has become a supportive stepsister to her little brother, Dwayne III. Soon after came Lennox, and finally Neal, daughter to Wayne and Nivea, born just months later. Lil Wayne was said to be present at the birth and still plays an active role in raising his children.

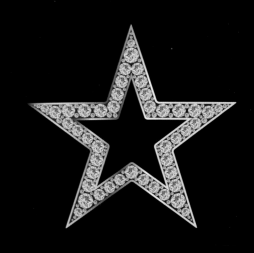

'I watch VH1 all day and I see these rich kids and they grow up and do nothing but just have VH1 cameras look for them at parties. I want my daughter and my sons to live like that.'

LIL WAYNE

> '...this is the first time that the album's leaked so close [to the release date]. Tha Carter III leaked two weeks before and we still did [1 million] the first week.'
>
> MACK MAINE

BACK IN THE GAME

The year 2010 wasn't the easiest for Lil Wayne. He was released from prison after serving an eight-month sentence at Rikers Island and reluctantly had to push back the release of his ninth album, *Tha Carter IV* (2011).

But Wayne, ever the stoic, was positive about his experience. He had survived time behind bars and he was ready to walk back into the limelight with his new album: older, wiser, sober (thanks to rules laid out by his probation officer) and back in the game. His first stop was his kids. 'Family first ... then back to business,' said Birdman when asked about his next project. But after a few weeks it was back down to business and the long-anticipated *Tha Carter IV*. Things didn't start well: just days before the official release, some tracks leaked online. It wasn't the first time.

GOOD YEAR FOR SOME

Lil Wayne declared he wasn't bothered about the leaked tracks. 'It just means people want to hear it,' he explained and pushed on with his promotion. The album was finally released digitally a few minutes after the 2011 VMAs in August 2011. And Wayne was right: it had 300,000 downloads in its first four days, going on to break the iTunes single-week album sales record, and to sell over a million copies and sell out his 'I Am Still Music' 2011 tour.

The following month, the rapper turned 29 years old and celebrated by finding out he had been listed in the 2012 *Guinness Book of World Records* for The Most US Hot 100 Hits By A Rap Artist – he has had 64 hits since 1999. But what about these rumours circulating that *Tha Carter IV* was to be his last album?

THE END OF THA CARTER?

For a while, Wayne has said that he felt continuing his music career indefinitely would be unfair to his children. In 2011 he also revealed that *Tha Carter IV* may well be his final album, later adding that working in the music business requires far too much commitment for a father, something the public could never understand. When the media caught wind of the rumours, Wayne stepped in to confirm that his retirement was 'not imminent'; rather he would still record for a few more years. But he also had plans to expand the label and maybe launch a fashion line like Kanye West. But for now, he would concentrate on the music and, of course, his children. It was important to him that they had a very different upbringing to the one that he had – even if it made him the man he is today.

'All the gangsta rappers are happy, all the skateboard rappers are happy, all the white rappers are happy ... Everybody just happy to do music these days.'

LIL WAYNE

FURTHER INFORMATION

LIL WAYNE VITAL INFO

Birth Name	Dwayne Michael Carter, Jr
Birth Date	27 September 1982
Birth Place	New Orleans
Height	1.67 m (5 ft 6 in)
Nationality	American
Alter Egos	Lil Wayne, Weezy

DISCOGRAPHY

Albums & EPs

Tha Block Is Hot (1999)

Lights Out (2000)

500 Degreez (2002)

Tha Carter (2004)

Tha Carter II (2005)

Like Father, Like Son
  (with Birdman, 2006)

The Leak (EP, 2007)

Tha Carter III (2008)

Mr Carter (EP, 2009)

We Are Young Money
  (with Young Money, 2009)

Rebirth (2010)

I Am Not A Human Being (2010)

Tha Carter IV (2011)

Mixtapes

Da Drought (2004)

Da Drought 2 (2004)

The Prefix (2004)

The Suffix (2005)

Dedication (2006)

Dedication 2 (2006)

Blow (2006)

Da Drought 3 (2007)

Dedication 3 (2008)

No Ceilings (2009)

Sorry 4 the Wait (2011)

TOP 10 SINGLES

2004: 'Soldier' (Destiny's Child feat. T.I. & Lil Wayne,
US No. 3)

2006: 'Stuntin' Like My Daddy' (with Birdman, US No. 7)

2008: 'Lollipop' (feat. Static Major, US No. 1)
'A Milli' (US No. 1)
'Got Money' (feat. T-Pain, US No. 1)
'Mrs Officer' (feat. Bobby Valentino & Kidd Kidd,
US No. 2)

2009: 'Every Girl' (with Young Money, US No. 2)
'Bedrock' (with Young Money feat. Lloyd, US No. 1)

2010:	'We Are The World 25 For Haiti' (US No. 2)
	'Right Above It' (feat. Drake, US No. 1)
	'Roger That' (with Young Money, US No. 6)
	'6 Foot 7 Foot' (feat. Cory Gunz, US No. 2)
2011:	'How To Love' (US No. 2)
	'She Will' (feat. Drake, US No. 1)

AWARDS

BMI Awards

2009:	Urban Songwriter Of The Year
2010:	Urban Songwriter Of The Year
	Most Performed Urban Song Of The Year (various)

BET Awards

2007:	Viewer's Choice Award 'Stuntin' Like My Daddy' with Birdman
2008:	Viewer's Choice Award 'Lollipop' feat. Static Major
	Best Collaboration 'I'm So Hood (Remix)'
2009:	Viewer's Choice Award 'Can't Believe It' with T-Pain
	Best Male Hip-Hop Artist
	Best Collaboration 'Turnin' Me On' with Keri Hilson
2010:	Best Group with Young Money

BET Hip-Hop Awards

2000:	Best New Artist
2007:	Alltel People's Champ Award 'Stuntin' Like My Daddy' with Birdman
2008:	Best Hip-Hop Collaboration 'I'm So Hood (Remix)'
	Track Of The Year 'A Milli'
	CD Of The Year *Tha Carter III*

	Best Ringtone Of The Year 'Lollipop' feat. Static Major
	People's Champ 'A Milli'
2009:	Track Of The Year 'Every Girl' with Young Money

Grammy Awards

2009:	Best Rap Song 'Lollipop' feat. Static Major
	Best Rap Album *Tha Carter*
	Best Rap Performance By A Duo Or Group 'Swagga Like Us'
	Best Rap Solo Performance 'A Milli'

Source Awards

2000:	Best New Artist

Teen Choice Awards

2008:	Choice Rap Artist

ONLINE

lilwayne-online.com: Official site with news, shows, store and Twitter updates

www.lilwaynehq.com: Top site for all Weezy fans out there, including info on his tattoos

myspace.com/lilwayne: Check this site out for Tha Carter's latest songs, videos and tour updates

facebook.com/LilWayne: Check out Lil Wayne's latest writing on the wall

twitter.com/LilTunechi: Join the 3.75 million other followers at @LilTunechi

BIOGRAPHIES

Morwenna Ferrier (Author)

Morwenna Ferrier started working at *The Observer* in 2003 and left her role as a contributing editor to various *Observer* monthly magazines in 2010 to be New Music and Reviews Editor at *X Magazine*. Currently freelance, she now writes about popular culture for *The Observer*'s New Review and *The Daily Telegraph*, and has contributed to *Grazia*, *ES Magazine* and *The Guardian*'s Guide. She lives in London with her boyfriend and her cat.

Priya Elan (Foreword)

Priya Elan is a leading music and entertainment journalist. He has written for a number of publications including *The Guardian*, *The Times*, *The Financial Times*, *Mojo* and *Grazia*. He is currently the Assistant Editor of NME.com.

PICTURE CREDITS